Midpoint

A Memoir

PATRICIA ANGELES

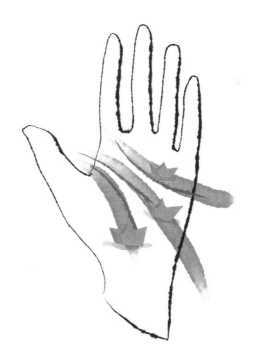

ISBN: 979-8-8478-8095-4

Disclaimer: This work depicts actual events in the life of
the author as truthfully as recollection permits. While all
persons within are actual individuals, names, and identifying
characteristics have been changed to respect their privacy.

For my daughters Maxine, Samara & Riley.
Because of you, I get to be me.

Contents

Foreword

—•—

M*idpoint* by Patricia Angeles presents an account of her major life milestones through a compilation of stories that represent failures, learnings, motivations, dreams, and unspoken thoughts.

While she believes that her stories may not resonate with everyone, she presupposes that every story deserves to be told. With her childhood stories starting in the Philippines to her adult life and immigration to the United States, Patricia reflects on her past as she plans her future. Through the recollections and ruminations, she debates whether her life has been a triumph or a tragedy or perhaps a bit of both.

As they unfold in her debut book, the life stories in Patricia's *Midpoint* offer thorough yet captivating details and insight to which I believe many, if not all of us, can relate!

Issam Ghazzawi, Ph.D.

Professor of Management

University of La Verne

Preface

I was twelve years old when I wrote my very first "book." It was about a group of young adults who decided to embark on an island holiday. In this lush and tropical setting, the story revolved around each character's first brush with love. Subconsciously, I was putting to paper everything I had hoped to experience when it was my turn to become a teenager. I laboriously wrote every word by hand on stationary folded lengthwise and bound it by staples. I was proud of my finished product, and the callouses I developed as a result of this exercise were worth it.

As I grew up, I always had this nagging desire to write an official book for publication. It was a silent, unchecked heavy hitter on my ever-growing bucket list. I wanted to write dystopian science fiction about a matriarchal society, exploring the impact of a role reversal between the sexes. Or an adventure story centered on two hitchhikers stranded in the Andes Mountains of Patagonia, the hostile Chilean terrain a focal point of the tale. For a time, I also considered writing a nonfiction book, a compilation of narratives about the lives of Philippine immigrants in the U.S. and their journey toward assimilation. Unfortunately, life kept me busy, and none of these progressed beyond the ideation stage.

In August of 2022, I visited the Getty Museum in Los Angeles and was left in awe at how one person could create such a resplendent, tangible, and lasting legacy that would surpass death. But I didn't have any fortunes to bequeath my daughters. I wondered how I could use my talents to achieve this same purpose. What was I good at? I could write. Yes. *That* I could do.

The main objective of this book is to give my daughters a glimpse of me in my truest essence and to communicate with them in ways I may not always be able to in the course of our daily interactions. Conse-quently, I hope, with these stories, to impart wisdom through the lessons I've learned during the first half of my life.

I am but a tiny speck in the grander scheme of things, and my experiences may not resonate with the masses, but I've always believed every story deserves to be told.

Midpoint is a collection of narratives I conjured from memory, an account of major milestones in my life and the people who have shaped me. These are stories that, while unique to me, represent the best and the worst of humanity.

To my daughters, Maxine, Samara, and Riley: My hope is, by reading this book, you will get to know me beyond motherhood and discover my many other layers—as a child, daughter, sister, friend, worker, and wife. In so doing, I hope that all three of you see a piece of yourselves in me.

Part 1: Manila

1984–2005

Starting Point

A s the last of the American Independence Day fireworks fizzled out during the summer of '84, a different type of celebration was happening at the maternity ward of Torrance Memorial Hospital: my birth as a tiny five-pound baby.

Remarkably small, I was told that my dad was initially terrified to pick me up and carry me in his arms. I was their first child after all, and having me on the cusp of their teenage years meant that as new and inexperienced parents, there was a huge learning curve to traverse.

Shortly after my birth, my parents decided to move back home to Manila. There were some business dealings to tend to and they agreed it would be best to raise me there.

I was the first grandchild, and everyone in the family took turns caring for me as my parents mapped out their future. My mom would eventually decide to go back to school to finish her last year of college, but my dad headed straight for the workforce, relinquishing his remaining years in optometry school.

When I was a few weeks old, my mom noticed that I was crying excessively despite being fed and lulled to sleep. I would wake up in the middle of the night, wailing nonstop for no reason. Helpless, my parents took me to my pediatrician, who performed extensive tests until I was diagnosed with a congenital heart defect. There was a small yet dangerously positioned hole in my heart. They were advised that the only treatment was by way of surgery. My paternal grandmother, or Lollie, as I would later call her, was a devout Christian. Instinctively, she turned to her faith, the one thing she knew she could count on. She mercilessly stormed the heavens with prayers, believing in her heart that it would make a difference.

During a checkup leading to the already scheduled surgery, the doctors, in sheer disbelief, confirmed that the hole had closed by itself. Without any material medical explanation, it was nothing short of a miracle.

This became my favorite bedtime story as I was growing up, trumping every fable and fairy tale my parents ever read to me.

The Pursuit
of Thinking

———•◦•———

In my earliest childhood memory, I was six years old. Perched on the potty while my dad was in front of the mirror, shaving in intense concentration.

Out of nowhere, I blurted out in Tagalog, "If and when you die, is there a way I can see you again?"

Caught off guard and not knowing how to respond to such a macabre question, he simply said, "It won't happen for a very long time, so let's not think about it, okay kiddo?"

Not long after, I redirected my interrogations to my poor mom. I plagued her with questions about the latest object of my obsession, the Leaning Tower of

Pisa, asking why it was in eternal suspension. Without any idea about the laws of gravity, in my young mind, I was already trying to make sense of it.

On the way to school, we would often pass by an area occupied by street kids selling floral necklaces and other trinkets to motorists and passersby. One day, it struck me that these kids, the majority of whom were much younger than I, were sleeping on the pavement with only the clothes on their backs. They were completely unprotected from the elements, while I got to lie down on a soft bed, surrounded by matching fluffy pillows.

Unable to reconcile this juxtaposition, I declared to my parents that from then on I would sleep on the floor, using a thin piece of cardboard as a pillow and a newspaper as my blanket. In my innocent heart, I wanted to internalize what it was like to be in their shoes. I kept on with this until my dad decided my little immersion experiment was enough. I moved back to my bed, but my rumination lingered.

For as long as I can remember, I have always been the type of person who takes time to reflect on the surrounding world, my thoughts often running deep. My brain is wired to constantly question and seek a richer meaning behind things.

I especially looked forward to my philosophy classes in college, where I would ensconce myself in the front row and allow my mental faculties to play at will. This served as my introduction into the lives of the best thinkers of our time—Epictetus being my personal favorite, one of the founding fathers of Stoicism, whose teachings I strive to live by to this day. Fully engrossed in lectures about free will, ethics, and the essence of being human, I aced these classes with a 1.0—the highest mark possible.

On one occasion, we were subjected to a personality test designed to determine our dominant temperament. I scored significantly high in the Melancholic quadrant. The results alluded to how I was never satisfied with superficial things and that I was constantly analyzing the past and contemplating the future. Further, it implied that I was emotionally sensitive, cynical, and a perfectionistic introvert.

In true scholarly fashion, I spent the rest of the day reflecting on that.

Playing Pretend

———•———

Most of my childhood was spent in Pasig City in Manila, Philippines. We lived in a townhouse complex where everybody knew one another. Our house was at the end of a cul-de-sac, making it the perfect spot for bored kids to congregate.

I was the lone girl in a brood of four. The rose among thorns. Back then, my brothers and I went to school in the morning until 4 p.m. and then headed home to take our afternoon nap or "siesta." After that, we would have a snack or "merienda," comprised mostly of Tender Juicy Hotdogs and white rice, pansit canton (Filipino stir-fried noodles), or Nissin Top Ramen partnered with Tang instant orange juice. Once revitalized by our hefty meal, we would run out to the streets and get into all sorts of mischief and adventures with the neighborhood kids until our caretakers yelled for us to come back inside for dinner.

Since my brothers and I were only two years apart, we had similar interests and enjoyed the same shows, like *Denver the Last Dinosaur, Duck Tales, Chip 'n Dale Rescue Rangers,* and our all-time favorite, *Power Rangers.* We would pretend to be our favorite characters and, altogether, we would "morph" into their animal counterparts. With much gusto, we would get into formation as we yelled, "Mastodon! Pterodactyl! Triceratops! Saber-toothed Tiger! Tyrannosaurus!"

Summer days were the best. We would stay outside, playing, from sun up to sun down, only returning home for meals, which we'd gobble up hurriedly in order to reconvene back outside and pick up where we left off. We would play endless games of tag, hide-and-go-seek, and Chinese garter. At the first hint of dusk, we'd grab our flashlights and hunt for ghosts while scaring each other with stories of haunted characters from Filipino folklore.

I especially looked forward to summer break because my dad's half-sister Julia, who was only a year older than me, would stay with us for the duration of it. She was my #1 accomplice and the closest I had to a sister. We were thick as thieves, always up to something.

Often, since we were older, we would gang up against my brothers by surreptitiously collecting things from them, such as erasers, pencils, stickers, and small toys. Once we had a sizable stash, we would sell the same items back to them in a sly attempt to milk them for their money, which we would then use for purposes amusing to us. We'd also cunningly design complicated obstacle courses that we knew would be challenging for the younger kids and their shorter extremities. As planned, we beat them all.

When we reached adolescence, Julia and I became so engrossed with the movie *Now and Then* and would watch it repeatedly, until we could recite the lines and sing the songs by heart. One day, our boredom led us to unearth my old Fisher Price toy radio. Copying the movie characters, we strapped it to my bike's basket using an old jump rope, blasted the soundtrack cassette tape, and sang our hearts out to Freda Payne's "Band of Gold" as we pedaled around town, the fresh breeze disheveling our hair.

During one of Julia's summer sojourns, I took her

to church camp, and without my knowledge, she introduced herself using an alias just for kicks. For one whole week, I struggled to keep a straight face whenever I had to call her by her new name! One time, we completely lost it and dissolved into uncontrollable fits of laughter while the people around us stared in confusion.

At the conclusion of camp, we found out that the alias had spread throughout the church, and my dad was interrogated by some of the elders who had discovered this double identity. We ended up being grounded for a week for intentionally misleading the congregation where my dad was an active and well-respected member.

It was a much simpler time. Kids were easier to please. There was no Internet, no social media. We were mostly left to our own devices, and we had to find ways to amuse ourselves. This kind of environment fostered creativity. It prompted our imagination to run wild and unfettered.

There was no fear of being kidnapped nor any ill-intentioned strangers lurking around as there are today. We were young and carefree, oblivious to the dangers of the real world. To have experienced this kind of freedom and then have a trove of happy childhood memories is a gift I hold dear. You can't really put a price tag on that.

As a grown-up, I wish it were as simple as morphing into our old favorite characters as a means to escape life's many curveballs.

Gill-ty

———•◦•———

Despite my adventurous streak, I was an obedient child. In fact, with full confidence I can proclaim that, between me and my brothers, I was the one who gave our parents the fewest headaches.

An episode occurred when I was in second grade. I was at home for a play date with my then best friend, Corinne, and was somehow dared into stealing our neighbor's fish. His house was about four doors down from mine, and he had a big, colorful aquarium in his open-door garage. All I had to do was scoop up one fish, any fish, and bring it home.

I looked around to survey my surroundings and saw that there was no one else in sight. I decided to act quickly. Without much trepidation, I went on to complete my dare.

I ran back home, clutching the poor fish as it flapped up and down, gasping for air. I could tell that it wasn't going to live much longer. As it took its final breath, I was momentarily struck with a sudden wave of guilt. We then flushed its limp, lifeless body down the toilet, thinking we had just literally gotten away with murder. Swearing to keep mum about what had just transpired, we innocently went on with our day, the fish and its unceremonious funeral forgotten.

A few hours later, we heard a knock on the front door. It was my neighbor, the fish's owner. Apparently, somebody had caught us in the act and notified him of our transgression. That fish I stole, he claimed, was special, of a rare kind. Not only that, but it was also pregnant and poised to breed.

My dad promised he would talk to me and impose appropriate disciplinary actions. Furious, he stomped up the stairs and proceeded to my room to scold me in a voice I'd never forget. Then, he escorted me to our enraged neighbor's house, where I offered an apology with tears in my eyes, repentant for my foolishness.

In my desperate need to prove myself and out of fear of losing my friend, I had succumbed to the pressure and ended up making a poor choice. This incident, seemingly insignificant at that time, would influence how I would later on respond to bigger peer-pressure scenarios, strengthening my moral compass in the years to come.

My Childhood Battle Scar

———◦———

Of the many family trips we embarked on, one would remain etched in my memory. I was eight years old, and we'd driven down to Los Baños, Laguna to avail of the hot springs the area was known for due to the geothermal heat and steam released from the nearby dormant volcano, Mount Makiling.

We crammed into an old four-door Toyota sedan, all of us kids plus two nannies. The trunk was packed to the brim with a week's worth of luggage, and the overflow had to be placed with us in the backseat— small bags on our laps and kitchen appliances tucked among our tangle of feet.

My mom was infamous for lugging her trusty rice cooker wherever we went, since Filipinos are big (white) rice eaters. For her, no meal is complete without rice. In fact, she'd frequently confess that in the event of an emergency, she would leave everything else behind, save for the rice cooker—and she really meant it. Beside my feet was the portable water kettle, a small appliance that ran on battery. A necessity for making coffee and tea for the grown-ups and warm milk for the kids. Bored on the way there, I started to mindlessly play with the buttons. When we finally got to our destination, my attention shifted and excitedly, I ran out of the car with the others to explore my new surroundings.

Later that afternoon, as we piled back into the still packed car to head out for a grocery run, I opened the door to take my usual seat in the back. Then, I leaned forward, hand outstretched, using the top part of the kettle for balance as I maneuvered my way in.

I accidentally pressed the dispense button, with my right foot directly underneath the spout. Boiling water hit my skin, and I screamed in agonizing pain. Horrified, my parents plucked me from the car, inspecting every part of my body for damage.

At this point, the pain had rendered me mute, but I distinctly remember one of my uncles pointing frantically toward my ill-fated foot. Later, he described to us how he saw before his very eyes the actual churning of flesh.

I was rushed to the nearest hospital, where I was treated promptly, but the burn had already overtaken the entire front part of my right foot.

In the weeks that followed, my nanny was tasked with changing my bandages. I would writhe in pain, squeezing her arm as she meticulously dressed my wound. Every night, right before I slept, my mom would religiously apply salve, hoping to minimize the scarring.

Over time, the wound closed, and as my foot grew, the scar shrank. It became my one and only battle scar from childhood and what I think of as the root cause of my helicopter parenting tendencies.

Barbies vs. Books

My love affair with books started the day I turned eight years old, thanks to the brilliant storytelling of Francine Pascal. My parents took me to a novelty toy store to get me my birthday gift: the newly released Malibu Barbie I'd been pining over. While in line to pay, I saw a stack of *Sweet Valley Kids #1: Surprise! Surprise!* books on display at the cash register and made a last-minute decision. I grabbed a copy and announced to my surprised parents I was choosing it over the Barbie for my birthday gift. That night, I consumed the book in one sitting, and that was all it took for me to become hooked. I would wait patiently for the next book in the series and hound my parents into buying it for me as soon as it came out. I ended up owning the entire collection.

I considered my books precious possessions and asked my mom to wrap them in clear covers and place name labels inside each one. I would organize and re-organize them in my bookshelf. Sometimes by numerical order, sometimes according to color, and sometimes by order of my favorites. At random times, I'd flip through the pages and savor the bibliosmia.

I read each night until the lights went off, and once I was sure everyone else was asleep, I'd bring out the mini-flashlight I kept hidden under my pillow and read beneath the covers until sleep found me. This eventually took a toll on my eyesight, and soon enough, I developed astigmatism. I ended up wearing thick eyeglasses that I couldn't see without. Eventually, I underwent LASIK surgery, the best investment I've ever made, which returned to me the clear vision I enjoy to this day.

Like many others, reading was my way to escape. And as I matured, so did my literary choices. Aside from the *Sweet Valley* series, I explored other beginner chapter books like *Babysitters Club, Nancy Drew Mysteries,* and *The Bailey School Kids.* I eventually moved on to YA novels, coming-of-age stories, and teenage romance.

In high school, I got my hands on Lois Lowry's *The Giver*. It was my first foray into my favorite genre, dystopian science fiction, and the most impactful book of my youth. I read the works of George Orwell, H.G. Wells, Mario Puzo, Sylvia Plath, and Chuck Palahniuk and discovered my affinity for Latin American writers, thoroughly enjoying the wistful writing of Paolo Coelho, Pablo Neruda, Laura Esquivel, Gabriel Garcia Marquez, and Isabel Allende.

In college, school textbooks got in the way of leisure reading, but I remember picking up *The Da Vinci Code* at some point and falling in love with Dan Brown's writing style. I've read all his books ever since.

Nowadays, I find myself drawn to historical fiction, specifically stories about World War II, the Holocaust, Nazis, the Third Reich, labor camps, and kapos. Stories about a time when the thin line between life and death was defined by a Fascist regime persecuting dissidents and Jews, Roma, homosexuals, labor leaders, Communists and Jehovah's Witnesses, all in the name of purporting to be some superior race.

Despite the inhumane atrocities that occurred, their stories are interwoven with threads depicting how the human spirit ultimately prevailed. With the number of living Holocaust survivors quickly dwindling—only a handful are still alive now, seventy-five years after liberation—I strongly feel it is our duty as readers of literature and history to pass down their narratives and to help inform the public's consciousness about the scars of our past. Of the many accounts I've read, *We Were the Lucky Ones, Auschwitz Lullaby*, and *A View Across the Rooftop* are my top favorites.

In recent years, I also started to delve into memoirs. I enjoy reading about other people's life trajectories and identifying resemblances between their stories and mine. *Shoe Dog* by Phil Knight and *The Ride of a Lifetime* by Robert Iger are my favorites from this category.

Reading remains a big part of my life. From getting me through my youth to being my saving grace during the onset of the coronavirus pandemic in 2019. Through it all, I learned that as long as there are books, I'll make it out fine.

Word Nerd

—•—

An immense love for words would soon be born out of my love for reading, and as I became exposed to more literary genres and various writing styles, I slowly developed my own and found my creative outlet through composing poetry and prose.

As a pitfall of growing up, from about age ten upward, I slowly developed social anxiety. I became reticent and started harboring insecurities. I refused to have my picture taken, and I'd shun opportunities to make new friends.

What started as a hobby of jotting down the day's events soon became a lifestyle. And since I am a creature of habit, I ended up with a journal entry for almost every single day of my life from sixth grade all the way up to high school, with occasional entries throughout college.

My writing abilities shone in school, and whenever we had group projects, I was always tasked with the writing component. I wrote my own college applications and assisted friends with theirs. I penned school papers in the black market, charged a fee, and used the meager profits to add to my budget for daily expenses. One time, I took on more work than I could handle. Not wanting to compromise my clients' orders, I paid someone else from a rival school to do my own paper. When I received the final version, I couldn't help but pick it apart. That night, I gave up sleep as I worked to revise the whole thing.

In my senior year of college, I composed yearbook blurbs for twelve of my peers. Word got around, and my crush, who had previously paid no attention to me, was suddenly friendly. When he approached me to ask if I could write his blurb too, it all suddenly made sense. My friends then joked that had we known it was my writing that would finally make him notice me; I should have written him secret missives a long time ago. All in the name of fun, of course.

Through writing, I am able to compose my thoughts better, and I like the process of organizing them into a finite structure. I enjoy conjuring up imagery during my frequent and sporadic daydreams and translating them into stories. Before the era of mobile phones, whenever I was in the middle of an important task and would come up with an idea or a concept to write about, I'd take scrap papers, unused napkins or anything I could write on and scribble them down.

I've discovered that, whenever I am troubled or anxious, I pen my feelings and somehow everything feels lighter. I am able to breathe a little better. Through writing, I found the voice I lost somewhere along the path to growing up.

Sacrosanct Sundays

———•◦•———

It's true what they say: little girls tend to gravitate more toward their dads.

Perhaps there is a biological explanation behind that, but for me, it was because my dad was the person who was visibly present. My dad is many things, but I'd say he is best known for his sense of humor. Living in a household permeated by his antics is the reason why I have such high expectations when it comes to jokes and am quick to judge mediocre attempts by people who think they are being funny.

I inherited his love for music and grew up to records of Swing Out Sister, Gloria Estefan, Sybil, and The

Carpenters playing repeatedly in the background—the soundtrack of my adolescence.

My dad is very charismatic, a true people person. I remember tagging along on his errands, and more often than not, it would take us double the time to get from point A to point B because he'd recognize someone he knew along the way, and they would end up chitchatting. Some say he has the makings of a politician—well-loved by all, extremely personable, a natural people connector, a kindred spirit.

He was legendary in our subdivision for his basketball skills, and our family name, Sayson, was synonymous with the sport. Playing ball was part of his daily routine, and our house was always bustling with activity whenever he had a big game. On these special occasions, his teammates and good friends, who also happened to be our godfathers, would often wind down at home after each match. Win or lose, we would share meals together as the kids listened to the grown-ups swap stories and recount a play-by-play of that day's game. Sadly, I did not inherit his athleticism, and sports never became my strongest suit.

He valued family and was big on traditions. As a rule, Sunday was strictly family day. No matter what activities we had going on during the week or how late we'd stayed up on a Saturday night, he would turn on the radio at 7 a.m. every Sunday morning and crank up the volume. It was his own unique way of waking us up for church service, which was always followed by family lunch.

His adamance about this rule was praiseworthy. No absences were allowed, and no excuses were accepted. For him, this was our only time to connect with one another, especially once we were teenagers, each buried in our own worlds and emotionally siloed.

My family is not perfect. We are not affectionate, and we could go days without talking to each other. But whenever we do reunite there are no awkward silences. In fact, you'd be hard pressed to get a word in. Our foundation is solid, our bond unbreakable. A large part of this is because of our Sunday family tradition. Looking back, I'm thankful my dad imposed this upon us for as long as he did.

Without putting it into words, he impressed upon me the greatest lesson I would learn from him. That very few things matter more in this life than having a happy family. In full partnership with my mom, he only had to live by example. And when I had a family of my own—Disney songs playing repeatedly in the background as the soundtrack of my children's childhood—I quickly caught on.

Savage Love

As my dad made his staggering presence felt, my mom hovered calmly and quietly behind his shadow. Unlike most moms, she wasn't big on affection or words, but one thing was clear—she was fiercely protective of her brood.

When I got into a brawl with one of the neighborhood kids, Cecilia, who deflated my bike wheels for no reason but to poke fun at me, I came home crying to my mom. Instead of dealing with the issue like a mature adult, she grabbed the water hose and, while pretending to water the plants, "accidentally" aimed it toward Cecilia, soaking her from head to toe.

When I was much older, my mom knew that one of my friends (who was also occasionally my enemy) would often pick on me. When this girl visited our home, my mom opened the door and told her, "Why are you here? I'm sorry, but you are not welcome here," sending her back home.

My mom can be quite the savage but is as real as they come.

Despite her brash ways, she did everything for us. She prepared our food (even going so far as peeling and deveining shrimps for the entire family!) and helped us kids with our schoolwork. She was overly competitive too; she would make sure we showed up at school with the most intricately made projects, worthy of being selected for exhibits. When I got into a cross-stitching phase, she would take me to the crafts store and allow me to buy all the materials I needed without any budget; the sky was the limit—an extravagance for someone as stingy as her. When I was obsessed with Jennifer Love Hewitt and Dawson's Creek, she helped me write countless fan mail and postmarked them to be sent out via air transport.

Though she rarely said it, these were some of the little ways in which I felt her love.

The strength of my parents' marital bond was apparent throughout their partnership. In fact, I don't recall a single instance of a major fight. They would bicker and argue, but my dad never raised his voice nor lifted a finger towards my mom. My mom's submissiveness probably had a lot to do with this harmony. Their peaceful, easygoing relationship became my standard growing up. It influenced my belief that having calm and logical discussions to resolve conflicts is the most effective approach, but when I got married, I realized that, unlike my mom, I needed my voice to be heard.

Experimental
Juice Concoctions

————◆•◆————

One woman who would teach me to use my voice was Lollie, an influential figure in my life right from the day I was born and while I was growing up. As a woman during the 1970s, she courageously packed up her belongings and flew to New York City with her scant savings, which was just enough to keep her afloat for a few months. She found an entry-level job in a department store and eventually worked her way up.

She was highly adept at managing finances, and with her earnings from the U.S., she returned to Manila and put up several income-generating businesses. She had a sixth sense when it came to entrepreneurship. She always knew what industry to dabble in, what product to sell, and once she had an idea, she would pour her heart and soul into executing it. There wasn't anything she couldn't do.

Her steely strength and single-minded determination to protect and provide for her family never wavered even after she became widowed.

Lollie financed my brothers' and my education, making sure we were placed in the best schools in the city. As I was the first grandchild, she doted on me, taking me with her as she traveled around the world. And during these trips, she taught me her ways of life.

She was a big health buff. During one of her phases, she came home with a juicer and experimented by mixing different fruits, then forcing us to drink her concoctions. We weren't allowed to leave the dining table until we finished them, bottoms up.

The problem was that her concoctions weren't exactly enticing to the taste buds. Pineapple + papaya. Melon + jackfruit. Durian + atis (Philippine Sweet Sop and Sugar Apple). We would struggle to drink those dang juices. My younger brother Marvin once had the bright idea of dumping his juice in the toilet and flushing it down while no one was looking. He got caught red handed, and as punishment, he had to drink double his serving.

Lollie and I shared a room. She often came home from a hard day's work at midnight to find me still up and studying, notes scattered all over her bed. I had to then gather all my stuff and move it to the trundle underneath hers to continue whatever I was working on. She slept with the lights on, accustomed to the sound of my school papers rustling and pens scribbling.

She taught me to carry myself with panache and signed me up for personality development classes to help boost my confidence and set me up for success. She was a staunch supporter of the dance community, a patron of the arts, and year after year, she invested in my brothers' and my cultural refinement by religiously taking us to watch ballet at the Meralco Theater during holiday season. The classical music accompaniment was her favorite. In my periphery, I'd sometimes catch her closing her eyes, bobbing her head to the melody. The shows often ran past my bedtime, yet not once did I ever need to fight sleep. And though I never desired to be a ballerina and have no musical inclination, many years of observation have taught me how to appreciate a great performance when I see one.

The first time I had my heart broken, I was devastated and cried for days. My dad, instilling tough love, urged me to toughen up and move on. "Malayo yan sa bituka!" (far from the intestines) he would often say—a Filipino idiom meant to convey that if the pain is far away from one's vital organs, it is considered insignificant and thus, bearable. When that didn't work, he reverted to comedy, his forte, by pointing out physical imperfections of the culprit who had caused my tears. My mom, always his silent supporter, just stood by nodding her head in perpetual agreement.

Lollie? She booked me the first flight out to Singapore, called her friends who lived there to arrange for my lodging and commissioned them to take me out. She dropped me off at NAIA Airport with a tight hug and a thick wad of crisp bills. Her parting words were, "Please go enjoy yourself."

I did as instructed and met up with a friend who took me around town. We partied at the famed upscale Zouk Nightclub, went shopping at Changi and Bugis, and stuffed ourselves with delicious Asian street food, hopping from one hawker center to another. I went home revitalized and with a brand-new realization: there was much more to life than my heartbreak. The world had more pressing problems. And though the pain was still there, it had subsided into something more like a dull ache that somehow didn't sting as much.

Alter Ego

———————•◦•———————

I went to a small private, all-girls Catholic high school, and my years there would be heavily defined by the emergence of cliques. Despite its size, our school did not lack in diversity, and a handful of groups stood out—the popular ones, the artists, anime lovers, the geniuses, and the troublemakers. I didn't belong to any group exclusively and considered myself a floater, drifting from one group to the next, mostly flying under the radar. Yearning for acceptance, I underwent several identity crises as I tried to figure out where I fit in the social hierarchy.

Growing up under the care and tutelage of strict, old-fashioned parents and a dad that was always a step behind in the leniency department didn't really help my cause. For the longest time, I wasn't allowed to attend social gatherings where boys were invited—school-sanctioned or not—but I was resourceful and found workarounds and loopholes to this rule. When my dad finally allowed me to go out and attend parties, he would drive me to the venue himself, drop me off, park the car, and sleep inside while waiting for me.

During my junior prom, my dad demanded that he meet my date prior to prom night, much to my chagrin. This guy was an acquaintance, and although we revolved around the same social circles, we were practically strangers. How was I supposed to tell him that my dad wanted a full-fledged meet-and-greet session? He turned out to be a trooper with endless patience, which was evident as my parents pried about his life with the level of precision usually reserved for fiancés. I was mortified but knew that if I didn't go through with it, there was no chance I would be allowed to attend, so I unwillingly compromised. As if that wasn't enough, my mom booked a room at the same hotel where we had our prom, making sure they could keep a close eye on me at all times.

I wasn't allowed to wear revealing outfits, either: no Daisy Dukes and backless tops. Being the more reasonable one, my mom slowly became my co-conspirator. As she herself had gone through the same strict rules, she understood my motives and knew that I just wanted to experiment with fashion and express myself freely by asserting my own clothing choices. Once, she tossed me a jacket on my way out to conceal the spaghetti straps of my party dress, in order to avoid my dad's judgmental eyes.

I was an awkward teenager who wore thick eyeglasses and braces. I also had unruly hair, which was quite impossible to tame. For a time, I struggled intermittently with body-image issues. I was five foot one and weighed ninety pounds yet still felt I needed to lose weight. I plastered pictures of skinny runway models on my bedroom wall, skipped lunch breaks with my friends, and resorted to crash diets.

I was the classic late bloomer, and by the time I became remotely aware of my looks, my peers had already started dating. Slowly, I began to pluck my eyebrows and ditch my glasses for contact lenses. I experimented with make-up and took a keen interest in the latest trends.

It was a time when teen fashion magazines were all the rage. One particular publication had a huge cult following and became every teenage girl's style bible. But as most girls clamored to be featured as models, attending go-sees, and sending in their best headshots, my dream was to write for them.

I was fifteen years old when I looked up the contact information of the editor-in-chief, a nice lady named Tina, and boldly mailed her a sample piece. She called my home phone and asked if we could sit down for an interview.

Shoot! I had no way of doing this without my parents finding out. Scared of the possible repercussions, I apologized and made up an excuse as to why I couldn't meet face-to-face.

The following morning, she called me back and said they would like me to conduct an already scheduled interview with a popular on-screen romantic couple. She went on to ask, if I couldn't make it to their location, would I be open to someone else doing the interview, after which the transcript could be forwarded to me, so I could still write my piece? Not knowing what I was getting into, I agreed.

The raw interview transcript and tape recording

were delivered to me at the school gate. That same night, I wrote up the article under the alias "Bianca Zialcita" (Bianca being a name I had pre-selected for my future daughter and Zialcita was the surname of my crush) and faxed it over the following day. It ended up in the next month's edition as a three-page story.

It became my little secret, the first official validation of my writing abilities. A silent nod of approval and a gateway to a future of endless possibilities.

The Burden of Choice

————— •◦• —————

In Manila, at least during my teenage years, there were only a select number of universities to pick from. All of us gunned for the top ones. Of the four that I applied to, I was accepted into a BS Biology program at De La Salle University (DLSU) and into the School of Liberal Arts at University of Asia and the Pacific (UA&P). Then came the tough part, how would I decide? Was I fated to be a DLSU Green Archer? Or a UA&P Dragon?

For context, I've always wanted to be a doctor. My dad's sister, who was also my godmother, or *Ninang* in

Tagalog, was a geneticist, and my grandfather, Lollie's husband, used to take me for a ride on a commuter bus to pick her up while she was on duty. As I quietly observed the flurry of hospital life, white coats swishing in the corridors and heels clicking on the floor, I felt a certain sense of belonging, cementing my dream of following the same career path. And so, imagine my elation upon receiving DLSU's acceptance letter.

My parents were equally happy, but evening came, and as the excitement simmered, my dad called me to the living room for a talk. He explained how they didn't feel comfortable with the idea of me making the trip to DLSU every day (about a two-hour drive from our house). Getting a dorm was out of the question.

Lollie then artfully segued into how she preferred that I, the eldest grandchild, prepare to take on the family businesses comprised of several food carts and a private school. UA&P had a competitive management program and was only a ten-minute drive away, making it very convenient to come home during long breaks to rest.

Back then, I didn't think much of it. I held the distinction of being the golden child and felt highly obligated to meet the aspirations of the elders in my family. In addition, one of my best friends since elementary school was bound for the UA&P too. Hence, it was set.

On orientation day, I excitedly stepped into the very modern campus, eager to start a fresh chapter. As expected, I eventually picked Management as my specialization.

During this time, my dad finally eased his restrictions and relented to a more reasonable curfew. I compensated for the deprivation I felt in years past by seizing every opportunity to go out. After school, my friends and I would flock together for drinking sprees, masked under the guise of group study sessions. Here, I learned how to chug like one of the boys, choosing beer over cocktails. On weekends, I took the occasional out-of-town, overnight trips with the gang.

Recently, I was asked what occupation I originally wanted to pursue, and I was reminded of this story. What would the trajectory of my life have looked like had I gone to DLSU? I will never really know. When you think about the gravity of it, the burden of choice, it's a tough pill to swallow. But the way I see it, every day we are faced with choices ranging from mundane to life-changing, and the moment we pick one over the other, we release all the possibilities that come with the unpicked one. All we can do then is make the most out of the path we do select and trust that we've chosen well.

Looking back, I believe things fell right into place. I was exactly where I was supposed to be—right smack in the dragon's pit.

Marching Toward the Future

———— ◆•◆ ————

B efore I knew it, I was marching up to the stage, about to be handed my college diploma. It was a bittersweet moment since it also meant I was soon bound to leave Manila for good.

It had always been the plan for our family to immigrate to the U.S. after we finished our studies. There would be more opportunities for all of us in the States, and we had kin based here. Initially, I had no qualms about it.

What I didn't expect was becoming so attached to my friends, especially during the last two years of college, since I was with them virtually 24/7. The thought of leaving them was unbearable.

Immediately after college graduation, we took our much-anticipated senior trip. A big group of us flew to Boracay, an island in the south of Manila, a popular vacation spot famous for its powdery white sand, crystal-clear waters and bustling nightlife.

This was our last hurrah, a celebration of our collective successes, and a final get-together before each of us went our separate ways. We rented a big house and spent our days island hopping, feasting on fresh seafood, watching the most beautiful sunsets as we lounged by the shoreline, and of course, partying. In Ryan Philippe's famous words from the '90s suspense flick, *I Know What You Did Last Summer*, it was the last summer of immature adolescent decadence.

The final few days in Manila arrived all too soon, and it was time to pack my bags—something I had avoided until the last possible moment. How would I fit twenty years of possessions in just two boxes? How do I begin to pick and choose what to take with me? I knew it wasn't possible and I was bound to leave something important behind, but, applying my best effort, I took on this emotionally difficult task.

On the day of my departure, I paused and took a long, hard look at my room, my sanctuary, which was now half-empty. Its walls bore the tangible marks of my life thus far. Holes where pictures had once hung, accidental scribbles from when I was a child, and scraped paint from when I constantly rearranged furniture depending on my mood. I had it painted purple back when it was my favorite color, and when I grew up and my preferences changed, I never really thought to update it. In hindsight, it was probably my own secret way of holding on to a childhood that went by too fast.

With tears streaming down my face, I bade my friends and loved ones goodbye. Hugs were exchanged and promises made to stay in touch. For one last time, I walked out of our family home and into my future.

Part 2: Los Angeles

2005–PRESENT

The Pit

---•◦•---

I arrived in Los Angeles in June of 2005. Fresh from the tropics, I wore hoodies during the peak of the Southern California summer.

We stayed at Ninang's quaint bungalow, where I shared a room with my mom and my youngest brother. After recovering from jet lag, the next few days were spent getting acquainted with the neighborhood, opening bank accounts and cellphone contracts, as well as preparing for the California driver's exams. I aced the written portion with a perfect score, and my one mistake on the actual driving test was due to over-wide turns (which I have since artfully mastered). I then applied for credit cards to establish my credit, since here in the U.S., having a good credit score indicates strong purchasing power and attests to one's credibility in honoring financial obligations.

My very first credit card was from Macy's. It had a $500 limit, and I used it to update my wardrobe, ensuring I had basic pieces for all four seasons.

This was something foreign to me. In the Philippines, it was mostly summer all year round, with a month or two of constant downpour—which meant our wardrobe didn't change all that much.

These activities temporarily helped curb my severe homesickness, but every day I would beg my parents to send me back home. My main argument was that I didn't need the opportunities available here in the U.S. If only I was given a chance, I would be equally successful in Manila. Each time, I was rejected.

Since I now had the essentials to start my life here, there was only one thing left to do: find a job. I started scouring job sites on the Internet, walked into physical stores and office buildings handing out my printed resume, and even went to a job agency. I attended job fairs and was invited to a handful of interviews, but my heart wasn't in it and I wasn't giving my best, hoping I could still convince my parents to yield to my pleas.

When I wasn't job hunting, I was on social media or Yahoo Messenger, biding my time. Slowly, I found myself reconnecting with old friends and acquaintances from Manila who had also moved to L.A.

We frequented the clubs in Hollywood, like Les Deux, LAX, Tatou, and Vanguard, plus V20 in Long Beach. We had post-clubbing nightcaps at Koreatown and hookah sessions in Pasadena. During this time, I was getting an allowance, so I didn't really have the motivation to persist with my job hunting. I was living my best life.

I celebrated my twenty-first birthday by purchasing booze for the first time at Albertson's. When the cashier checked my ID and saw that it was my birthday, she rang up my purchase and said, "Happy birthday, hun. Welcome to the best years of your life." She would end up 100% on point.

As my one and only birthday wish, I appealed once more to my parents to let me visit Manila for a two-week vacation, and they acquiesced. Happy to be back in the company of my friends, I backslid to my old, carefree ways. Though I relished their company, I had an inkling that something had changed. I couldn't quite put my finger on it. Somehow, it no longer felt like the home I once knew. I even squeezed in a trip to Boracay, which was still beautiful, but strangely, had lost its old appeal. This peculiar feeling reminded me of a line from Sue Monk Kidd's masterpiece, *The Invention of Wings*:

> *"For a moment I felt the quiet hungering that comes inside you when you return to the place of your origins and the ache of mis-belonging. It was beautiful, this place, and it was savage. It swallowed you and made you a part of itself, or if you proved too unassimilable, it spit you out like a pit of a plum."*[1]

Unknowingly, I had become that pit, and deep inside, I was longing to fly back to L.A.

---

1. MLA. Kidd, Sue Monk. The Invention of Wings. New York :Viking, 2014

Bubbles

———•———

After a few more months of bumming around and enduring lectures and incessant prodding from my parents, I finally saw the light. There was no escaping it anymore. I needed to get a job like any self-respecting, responsible adult. I upped the ante on my job search and changed my approach. I started to leverage my small network.

In true Filipino fashion (which means a heavy reliance on connections), I was highly recommended by a family friend for an entry-level office administrator position at a dental clinic. The basic job duties included answering phone calls, scheduling appointments, and filing paperwork.

I showed up on my first day bright and early, ready to face whatever was thrown at me. The day went by quickly, and everything was a breeze. As I gathered my things, my supervisor summoned me to the restroom and explained how the staff took turns cleaning. Being the newbie in something akin to an initiation ritual, I was (surprise!) in charge for the day.

Without any semblance of emotion, she dumped the cleaning supplies and left me to fend for myself. Having neither the experience nor any idea of how to clean basically anything—and coming from a place and culture where it was the norm to have in-house staff do that for you—I was, suffice it to say, lost and overwhelmed.

However, not one to back down from a challenge, I rolled up my sleeves, put on some gloves, and started cleaning as best I could. Covered in soap bubbles and smelling like Windex, I found myself in disbelief that, with a bachelor's degree under my belt and an excellent academic record to boot, I was literally on my knees, cleaning other people's dirt. I felt that this task wasn't commensurate with the level of skill I could offer. Defeated, I couldn't help but cry.

I went home and complained to my parents,

who straightaway reprimanded me for my wrongful feelings of entitlement. News reached Lollie all the way in Manila, and since she was guilty of coddling me all those years, she started to blame herself for how I turned out. Wanting to put a stop to the escalating family drama and hoping to appease them all, I did what was expected of me. I sucked it up and stayed a few more months.

Up until that time, I had been in my own little bubble that needed to be popped. It was a rude yet much-needed awakening, and the most effective character building I'd experienced thus far. It humbled me and caused a seismic shift in my views on the dignity of labor. Not to mention, it is the reason why I'm now a better bathroom cleaner—although I'm positive my mom would be quick to disagree.

Ripped Jeans
and Flip-Flops

---•◦•---

After my stint at the dental office, I decided to apply for a retail job at one of my favorite clothing stores in a nearby mall, partly for the discount and also for a change of scenery. I attended a group interview where I was lost in a sea of teenagers—high school kids mostly. I stuck out like a sore thumb, but I confidently talked my way through and was hired on the spot. I had silent suspicions that my ethnicity worked to my advantage, as the company seemed to be doubling up their diversity efforts.

The brand epitomized the Southern California beach-and-surf culture, and as store representatives, the only requirement was for us to wear their brand during our shifts. I would show up in ripped jeans and flip-flops, reeking of their best-selling perfume, which I'd sprayed all over. I folded heaps of clothes between my fitting-room and go-back duties, fluttering around while waiting for my shift to end.

It was peak early 2000s, when emo/alternative music and indie bands dominated the scene. Their music, which played throughout the store the entire working day, resonated with me and perfectly mirrored a huge part of my personality: pensive, highly emotional, and broody. I was an extrovert party girl by day and an introvert emo girl by night. Songs from Taking Back Sunday, Paramore, Anberlin, and Acceptance blasted through my iPod earphones, while my journal entries included recurring themes of heartbreak and unrequited love.

I was paid a pittance, the majority of which went straight toward bus fare. Without a car to my name yet, my mom painstakingly taught me the local bus system. Every day, I walked to the bus stop and rode the Foothill Transit bus 492, which looped from El Monte to Montclair. My dad would cajole me that my pay wasn't enough to sustain the bus fare alone, but I was mostly in it for the experience.

I eventually made some friends and earned myself an invitation to a house party, which I attended without really knowing what to expect. There was some dancing, a little bit of mingling, and a whole lot of drinking. As the night progressed and the crowd thickened, it got disconcertingly loud, and people started getting rowdy. Before I knew it, police sirens were blaring and cops were pounding on the front door. Imagine being new to a country and having a run-in with law enforcement. They asked us partygoers to tone it down. Apparently, the neighbors were complaining about the noise. They checked IDs, wrote up citations and eventually left. This would be my official baptism by fire, an introduction to the local social scene. It also spurred me to rethink my priorities.

I viewed this incident as a reflection of my time at the clothing store – shallow, lacking in substance, and fun while it lasted. Shortly after, I tendered my resignation, stating that I wanted to pursue other opportunities. I was ready to see what was in store for me beyond the confines of the mall.

Taking One
for the Team

———•◦•———

My next job would be a drastic change in environment. From a clothing store that played deafening music, I transitioned to a small local bookstore, where we spoke in hushed tones to maintain the tranquil ambiance. My usual getup of open-toed shoes and casual T-shirts was now considered inappropriate.

It was a slow-paced job, and my responsibilities included manning the cash register, organizing the shelves, answering the phone, and helping out walk-in customers. There was a lot of down time, which I happily took advantage of by leafing through stacks and stacks of books. I got first dibs at new releases and even had the chance to meet one of my favorite authors, Shannon Hale, whose book, *The Goose Girl*, I had devoured as a tween.

My most memorable moment during my time there happened at the launch of a new *Curious George* book. We worked especially hard to ensure that everything would proceed without a hitch. I helped decorate the space with red and yellow balloons and made sure everything was spotless by running the vacuum cleaner repeatedly and lining up the chairs in perfect symmetry.

On the day of the event, the store began filling up with excited kids. As we were getting into position, ready to assist, we were called to the back room at the last minute. Our store manager informed us that the person who was tasked to don the Curious George costume was a no-show. She needed someone to step in, stat.

To this day, I still don't know what compelled me to do so, but I ended up taking one for the team. I shimmied into the bulky two-piece ensemble that was probably heavier than my entire body mass while my friends guffawed and snickered in the background. I took a deep, long breath and made my grand entrance.

I waved and danced, got kicked and stepped on, pushed and squeezed by kids of all sizes. All this while I was sweating bullets underneath. In what would be the longest hour of my life, I survived unscathed and with a newfound respect for the people doing such jobs for a living. When I became a mom, I strictly cautioned my kids to be extra careful and gentle around costumed characters.

The excess downtime at the bookstore job also allowed for some deep bonding with the other employees. Pretty soon, I started hanging out with them after work.

Once, on our way out for a night on the town, my friend's boyfriend who was driving turned out to be intoxicated. He started to lose control of the vehicle, swerving wildly on the 101 Freeway in the San Fernando Valley.

We all shrieked in panic. My friend, riding shotgun, was somehow able to take the wheel. The next thing we knew, we had exited the freeway and were aiming toward a parked car, which we grazed before we could stop.

We got out of the vehicle to assess the damage. My friend left her contact information on a Post-it note affixed to the scraped car's windshield.

Scared and shaken, I immediately called my dad, rousing him from sleep. He picked me up and brought me back home to safety. It was my first brush with real danger—and a wake-up call reminding me of my limits.

Our drunk driver apologized profusely to us the following day, but it was the last time I would ever fraternize with this group outside of work.

Jane Doe

———•◦•———

After my stint at the bookstore, I was hired as an entry-level consultant at a midsize management consulting firm. It was my first desk job, and my manager was an elderly Caucasian lady named Jane. Jane was an interesting character who showed telltale signs of being unconsciously racist. For the duration of my time under her purview, not once did I feel the support I needed to thrive in my role, and there was a clear disparity between the way she treated me versus my other colleagues. To be fair, she was never particularly hostile toward me, so I chalked it up to personality or possibly cultural differences.

The final straw happened when I had just returned to the office from a leave of absence. It was during our annual review period, and in the middle of what was already a tense discussion, she dropped the bomb: I was getting a 0% salary increase for the following year. I was stunned. In this industry, like many others, it's typical to get anywhere between a 0.5-3% increase contingent on the company's overall performance the previous fiscal year. Based on both experience and word of mouth, even the most unproductive employees never got zero unless it was an extreme behavioral issue. In addition, a performance report had just circulated indicating that the company had raked in significant profits, so naturally, everyone was expecting some type of incentive.

Subduing my initial reaction, I trod down the path carefully, keeping my emotions in check. I inquired about the factors that led to this decision. She stated it was simply because I had been gone for half of the year.

"All right," I said calmly. "What about the other half that I did work? It feels like, given the results of this review, my performance during that other half was blatantly disregarded."

Silence. I could tell she was taken aback. But instead of answering my question directly, she responded in a patronizing tone. "Wow, you are very brave to question this. But the decision is final, and there isn't anything I can do regarding this matter."

Revealing that she didn't expect this type of reaction from me only proved that she perceived me as someone who wasn't used to standing up for herself. Was I just stereotyped as a woman? Was it my ethnicity? As if that wasn't insulting enough, she was unable to supply a proper answer for my very valid question.

Our uncomfortable conversation eventually came to an end, but I wasn't going to take things sitting down. While I was reacting out of pure, raw emotion, I knew deep down that something was not right.

Immediately, I sprang into action. I bitterly perused the Internet and applied to other jobs, hoping to get out of that toxic environment. Next, I contacted human resources. I knew it was going to be an uphill battle fighting someone higher up, but if push came to shove, at least I had everything properly documented. I reported what had happened, putting my full trust in the company's non-retaliation policy. A preliminary investigation was conducted, but the case was ultimately shelved.

I don't regret fighting the good fight, even if I was unsuccessful in the end. I want my kids to glean that standing up for yourself is the best way to build your self-worth, something no one can ever take away from you.

Newspaper Clipping

I came home one afternoon to find my dad reading at the dining table.

He called me over and handed me a small newspaper clipping. It was an employment opportunity, a job opening at a Fortune 500 financial institution. Tired of hopping from one job to another, I needed some sense of stability. I was longing to start a lifelong career. He encouraged me to apply, and I grabbed it as excitement began to overtake me.

After polishing my resume, I sent it in and was invited for the first round of interviews. It ended up being a three-hour affair. Alongside my fellow applicants, I had to present a competitor study in front of a panel of interviewers consisting of high-ranking managers in the district. After that, we did a round robin of one-on-one interviews with these same managers.

I was dressed to the nines, decked out in my brand-new suit set from Express and shiny pumps from Nine West. I was confident in my command of the English language, since it was the medium of instruction in the Philippines. What I didn't know was that *formal English* (what we'd been taught) is distinctly different from *conversational English*. Not to mention, my Tagalog accent was very strong.

Still, I kept my insecurities at bay and acted like the professional I was trying to project. In the middle of my presentation, my laptop shut down completely, leaving me in the middle of my ten-slide PowerPoint deck. I calmly offered my apologies and proceeded to finish the report verbally from memory despite the fact that I was a big bundle of nerves the entire time.

Exactly four days later, I got a call from Laura, the human resources recruiter, with whom I've remained in contact to this day. She offered me a position in their banker-training program class that spring.

For seven weeks, my mom dropped me off at the Covina Metrolink Station, where I would take the train to Union Station in downtown L.A. Upon disembarking, I would run in heels alongside blue-collar workers, dressed sharply with my iPod in hand as I elbowed my way to the subway, which would take me to Seventh and Figueroa. From there, it was a five-minute uphill walk to the swanky high-rise, ground zero of my banker-training program.

I topped my class, besting thirty-four others, and I stayed at that company for the longest part of my career: fifteen years.

Two Weeks' Notice

Following my graduation from the banker-training program, I was placed in a local branch with the title of Personal Banker. My manager was notorious in the entire district as one tough cookie. She had earned a reputation as someone that would crack the whip unapologetically. Simply put, there was no messing around with this woman.

I went into a training period, getting acclimated to the banking nomenclature, systems, and corporate culture. But perhaps my most important learning, a true eye-opener, was that my job, as all others in consumer banking (branches), was truly and in essence a sales position. We had a daily goal that we had to meet and a certain number of checking, savings, and referrals that we had to open, or we would get added to the naughty list.

First things first. I am not a salesperson. I don't like being pushy, and I'd much rather work quietly on the sidelines. It was a highly competitive environment, and I was easily intimidated by my co-workers who all proved to be top performers constantly hitting their numbers. In the beginning, having no customer base and being the newbie, I struggled to keep up.

I was twenty-two years old and enjoying earning my own money, shopping to my heart's content, and going out with friends. I didn't have my priorities straight and lived day-by-day. In fact, my mom felt the need to step in and help me manage my finances by showing me how to save. When I turned twenty-three, I decided to throw this big birthday bash at a club: open bar, bottle service, unlimited guest list—the works. I ended up with a bill of $5,000, which drained my savings account. My mom was livid!

After much deliberation, I woke up one day and decided I was done with being a banker. I didn't want to deal with the pressure of sales goals anymore, so I crafted a long-winded two weeks' notice, pouring out my feelings and proclaiming that this line of work was not for me. I handed it to my manager, who read it on the spot.

She then looked me in the eye and ripped it into pieces! I was shocked. I had been mentally prepared to receive a lashing, a tearful closure maybe, but definitely not this. This was way beyond the realm of my expectations.

"Stop this nonsense and get back to work," she said matter-of-factly.

"Um...but I just resigned," I retorted.

"You're just overwhelmed. You'll be fine. Just do everything I say, and you'll make it to the top. I know you will. Trust me."

Reluctantly, I walked back to my desk, still in disbelief over what had just happened, but ultimately, I decided to give it another shot.

She became my very first mentor. We were the first ones in the office and the last ones to clock out, working closely together.

She treated me more like a daughter than a direct report, teaching me the ropes of banking, welcoming me into her home, giving me her hand-me-down business suits, and even offering sage advice on my personal and romantic life. I remain indebted to her for everything she taught and did for me.

Before long, I had my own clientele, consisting mostly of Filipino customers. They gravitated toward me since I fluently spoke and understood Tagalog, in which most preferred to conduct their dealings. I built good rapport with them, and some would visit the branch just to drop off food and gifts for me. I once had a delivery of fresh salmon transported from Alaska from a client whose son was a fisherman there. I would get invited to family celebrations and even unexpectedly received a marriage proposal—which I politely declined due to both conflict and lack of interest.

A year later, I emerged as a top performer in the district and was awarded at a lavish, all-expenses paid ceremony in Las Vegas. We were entitled to invite a guest. In my case, I brought my mom, who was only too eager to participate in the free trip.

We were treated to a shopping spree and received Visa gift cards and free iPods. As a bonus, we bumped into actress Jessica Biel during check-out and asked if we could take a picture. She obliged!

The Road
Less Traveled

———•◦•———

In 2006, when I was two years into my banking career, I was dating casually and enjoying meeting new people. Just as I was zeroing in on one particular guy, in the most dramatic twist of events, he disappeared without warning. I later found out that he had written a lengthy and very hateful public blog post meant to attack me as he felt I had led him on. To rub salt on my already stinging wound, he started dating one of my close friends.

Feeling blindsided, I needed a Singapore part deux. On a whim, I flew to Hawaii with a friend in a desperate act of escapism. We were out and about every day and made sure to hit all the tourist spots, leaving me little time to mope. I was grateful for the temporary distraction.

I arrived back in L.A. on a Saturday, physically and emotionally drained. I did a lot of thinking on the flight back and was still processing these thoughts when my friend Mike called, inviting me to go out clubbing that night. He wanted to introduce me to someone. Having nothing better to do and nothing to lose, I dragged another friend along, and off to Hollywood we went.

Enter Andre. He had walked into the club, loud and boisterous, as if he owned the place. We were casually introduced, and he briefly glanced my way without so much as a greeting before he moved on. I found this quite obnoxious and quickly decided I didn't have time for any of it. Little did I know, this inconspicuous meeting would be pivotal in changing the course of the rest of my life.

A week later, we went to dinner with the same group, and I finally got the chance to talk to Andre minus the loud clubbing music. During our conversation, I discovered that he was nothing like my first impression of him. We exchanged numbers, but I didn't hear from him for some time after that. Though I was dying to reconnect, my prideful self would not let me concede to his obvious mind games.

In the beginning of 2007, he finally sent me a text message:

"Hey Trish! Morning. How are you?"

It was the perfect way to start the new year and the first of what would be a lifetime of exchanges.

We went out and did the usual movie dates, romantic dinners, biking at the beach, clubbing with friends.

A few months in, we were hit with a big crisis that tested our budding relationship, and I was placed in a difficult position where I had to choose between him and my friends. He had gotten into a scuffle with Mike, our common friend that introduced us and whom I had known for years. Lines were drawn, and I was forced to pick sides. It was then that I realized what a huge part he already played in my life. I couldn't afford to lose him.

Andre was the first guy I ever had the courage to introduce to my very critical parents. When my dad disapproved of his clothing choice, long hair, and unshaven face during their initial meeting, my knee-jerk reaction was to feel defensive and protective. There would be more instances like this. Unconsciously, I was slowly overcome with a sense of responsibility for his well-being and wanted to protect him at all costs.

It didn't come to me in a rush like what I expected. I actually felt misled, because up until then, my expectations for love and romance were all hinged upon the books I'd read and shows I'd watched. Instead, it was a gradual realization, a progressive dawning.

Unlike most of our friends, we did not have a big, fancy wedding. There was no grandiose proposal, no public declaration of our undying love for each other. It was unplanned, a spur of the moment decision, an overwhelming feeling of being in the right place at the right time.

It happened on a cold and dreary December afternoon while we were on a holiday getaway in Las Vegas. In the middle of a deep conversation about life and love, we decided to get married. It didn't matter that we had only been together for less than a year. Suddenly, time was irrelevant. As passersby wheezed past us in the Strip, clad in multi-layered clothing, it felt as if everything was in slow motion.

After taking care of the paperwork, we went to an obscure place named Cupid's Chapel. We were dressed in the most casual clothing, but our hearts were full, worn proudly and firmly on our sleeves. Without either the presence or the knowledge of our family and friends, we exchanged I do's.

On the flight home, the magic wore off and reality slowly crept in. Sooner or later, I knew I had to tell my parents. On the day of reckoning, I remember fidgeting nervously as I confessed the story of our elopement, bracing for my dad's impending wrath. As expected, he was seething with anger, but more than that, he was heartbroken.

In traditional Filipino culture, what I had done was considered a sign of disrespect. It is customary for the groom to officially ask for his would-be bride's hand in marriage, and families from both sides are involved in the elaborate ritual.

We wrapped up our talk, and as we made amends, my dad assured me that he would have given us his blessing either way, as he was only ever after my happiness.

As a newly married couple, we lived in my parents' house and stuffed our collective belongings into one tiny room. This new dynamic came with its own set of challenges, but it also allowed my parents to get to know Andre better and vice versa. Before long, a mutual respect formed. Soon, that evolved into mutual affection, proving that time, thief that it is, can also sometimes be a gift, with its uncanny yet beautiful ability to heal scars and stitch broken pieces of the heart back into place.

Coming from two starkly different backgrounds and upbringings naturally yielded two distinctly contrasting sets of ideals and beliefs, making our adjustment period especially tough. Despite this, we had three things in common. In everything, we gave it our all. We kept trudging down the path, never looking back. Throwing in the towel was never an option.

Andre and I did everything together. We saw the world and made big financial decisions together. We tried to make sense of this new life, becoming bona fide adults, hand in hand. Unknowingly, we were also building a foundation that would prove to be highly beneficial in starting a family.

If I could, I would give my twenty-four-year-old self a big pat on the back for taking the road less traveled. By defying the expectations set by my parents when it came to the mechanics of a proper wedding and by turning a blind eye to traditional beliefs around an acceptable courtship period, I created my own destiny. Though I caused my family some pain, making these decisions for myself has ultimately led me to this beautiful life—imperfect as it is—that I wouldn't trade for anything.

Climbing My Way Up

⸻•◦•⸻

A long with building the foundation of my marriage, I was also slowly forging my own career path. After two-and-a-half years, I had maxed out my time being a banker and was recruited to join the company's Treasury division. I was jumping over the fence and fulfilling my dream of moving into corporate: no sales goals and no disgruntled customers to deal with.

As an implementation coordinator, I was assigned a portfolio of customers for whom I would set up treasury products and services. It was 70% data entry and 30% customer service, and I excelled at it. It was an exciting time for the company, and I took part in a pilot program implemented to test out the hybrid remote-work model.

I quickly climbed the ranks and earned a much-coveted award called Stellar Club Service, where I bested 200 of my peers. I was also promoted to a senior role and selected to join a prestigious program geared toward grooming the next generation for leadership positions through networking banquets and conferences in various parts of the country. These events allowed us to socialize and learn from our executive leaders.

As if my hands weren't full enough, I decided to go back to school. I enrolled in the University of La Verne's (ULV) MBA program, opting to specialize in international business. I worked in the morning and then made it just in time for my evening classes, which started at 6 p.m. At 10 p.m., Andre, who worked nearby, would pick me up from campus after his shift ended. We savored this time, driving home together. We'd stop by Circle K and buy all sorts of junk food that we'd binge at home as we watched our favorite TV shows, or we'd just park somewhere and talk about the day's events.

It's easy to fall into the trap of complacency, especially when you've mastered your job and are reaping the benefits of seniority. It was Andre who pushed me out of my comfort zone. With our common goal of getting our own place in mind, I targeted higher-paying jobs. I was then offered a role in Treasury sales, our sister team, but contrary to the title, it was not a sales-centric job. I would be in charge of preparing proposals, scheduling and attending client meetings, and collaborating with a consultant.

After a year, I was snatched up and offered a position in Treasury production support. The salary bump allowed Andre and me to move into our own place closer to my new office.

My years here were some of the most memorable in my career. A big chunk of my responsibilities included being on rotation for on-call duty during weekends and holidays to support product and service interruptions.

I remember getting paged one New Year's Eve and welcoming the New Year while triaging an issue involving a website that went down. I was also part of an all-hands-on-deck situation in several potential Distributed Denial of Service (DDoS) attack threats. Once, I was on the phone for close to ten hours as we tried to recover stuck wire transactions amounting to millions of dollars. It was grueling work, but there was never a dull moment. It kept me on my toes and trained me to make executive decisions on the fly.

By this time, I had become rather savvy at negotiating job offers. I knew my worth, and I spoke more brazenly during job interviews. Not long after, I was offered a job in the internal investigations division. After eleven years in Treasury, this would be my official transition into the fast-paced world of Risk.

In my new risk consultant role, I was in charge of creating reporting and metrics dashboards, providing support on system testing and code releases, and presenting quarterly reports to the management team. I stayed in this new job for two years, garnering awards and accolades.

While driving home from a brunch date with my girlfriends, I received a call from an internal recruiter offering me a role in the Operational Risk Transformation Office. I boldly counteroffered for a 30% salary raise plus 100% remote work. When the hiring team agreed, there was no turning back.

My move to the Risk line of business would also aptly reflect the evolution of my personal risk appetite. I was now making bigger career moves and became a little less hesitant to take the plunge.

Crossroads

---·•·---

My job in the Operational Risk Transformation Office introduced me to the best manager I've ever had the pleasure of working for. Aside from our similar work ethics, we were both type-A personalities: organized and highly analytical. She entrusted me with big projects and never failed to reward me or announce my accomplishments in front of the entire team. Under her leadership, I felt valued, appreciated…seen. She was also a mother and encouraged us to put family first. Being a stalwart believer in work-life balance, she was someone who actually put that into practice.

On year two of my stint, I was faced with a crossroad that questioned my integrity—which is one thing I take pride in both personally and professionally. I am a stickler for rules, and I'm usually afraid to break them.

When my integrity is questioned, I get defensive and will put up a fight without hesitation. As I had hoped, my unblemished record corroborated by my peers spoke for itself.

As a woman and minority in cutthroat corporate America, I've always known that I have to work twice as hard. There are times when I am the only woman in the room. Or sometimes, I'll be the youngest. Occasionally, my opinions are brushed aside and my thoughts disregarded. But I've met people who have cheered for my success, who pause in the middle of a heated discussion to ask me to weigh in. I've learned to keep them in my corner, thankful for their help in paving the way for me.

I've been belittled for being too ambitious and was once called out for working too hard, leaving no time for my children. As if being a mother means you have to give up on your own dreams. I refuse to be dragged down by this kind of mindset, and I'm here to break glass ceilings by showing my daughters that one can be a successful career woman and a great mother at the same time.

Work is such an integral part of my life, and the kind of mother I am now is a byproduct of the kind of worker I've evolved into. My quick decision-making, efficient problem-solving, and critical thinking are all traits I've developed and mastered in the workplace.

In April 2021, I reached an important career milestone, my fifteen-year anniversary with the company. It was on this occasion that I decided perhaps it was time to get out of my comfort zone once more and explore greener pastures. I got an incredible job offer from a competitor, another formidable financial institution, with everything I could ever hope for. So, I packed my bags and bade my old company goodbye.

My banking career was something I hadn't planned or foreseen. The universe conspiratorially dropped it on my lap and let me navigate from there on out. The passion didn't come naturally either. It came rather slowly. Intermittently at first before evolving into an enveloping feeling that consumed me, and at that point, I knew this was meant to be my life's work. One of my most fervent hopes is that when the time comes, my daughters will also stumble upon the things that spark their souls and make them feel most alive.

Motherhood Musings

———————•◦•———————

At age twenty-seven, I took a leap of faith into motherhood, not quite knowing what to expect. It was January 2011 when I found out about my first pregnancy.

Unfortunately, at five weeks pregnant, Andre and I lost the baby. Our medical team assured us there wasn't anything we could have done to prevent it; that the human body has a natural way of expelling whatever it suspects as unviable.

It wasn't too long until I got pregnant again. This time, I was more careful, more discreet, and I took extra precaution with every movement. The early stages were challenging. I threw up incessantly and lost a lot of weight.

Once I passed the first trimester mark, I started feeling better and eating more. As a first-time mom, I wanted to experience it all, starting with setting up the baby registry and carefully picking out each item, shopping for baby clothes, and selecting the perfect crib. I dragged Andre to hospital tours, and we attended Lamaze classes, read all the books, and tracked the baby's growth each week. I created a detailed birth plan and attended three baby showers hosted by family and co-workers. At six-months pregnant, I was already planning the baby's first birthday.

On December 11, 2011, Maxine Adrienne was born. My labor progressed very quickly, and by the time the anesthesiologist entered the delivery room to administer the epidural that I had begged for the moment I set foot in the hospital, it was too late. I was already crowning. She came out at 8:11 a.m., all six pounds of her, this tiny little thing with the roundest, most alert set of eyes I had ever seen.

It was a smooth adjustment to motherhood, and Andre truly stepped up to his role. Together, we navigated this new chapter, giving up vices from our youth and embracing the unknown.

Maxine was an easygoing child. I only remember one tantrum throughout her toddler years, and it was because we had to wake her up and take her out of the stroller to pass through airport security. She was a social butterfly, this little girl of mine, and she loved talking to people. At eleven months, she was already reading sight words and turned out to be a voracious reader like me.

I got pregnant with our second child when Maxine was three, but this pregnancy was a whole new ballgame—definitively different from my first.

During the early weeks of my first trimester, I was diagnosed with hyperemesis gravidarum, a severe form of nausea and vomiting during pregnancy. I was bedridden for the first three months and lost thirty pounds, since I could not keep anything down, water included. I also had gestational diabetes, which required me to test my blood sugar three times a day. As a result, my fingertips would often bruise. I was on medical leave early on in my pregnancy due to these conditions and relished the extra time I got to spend with Maxine.

I still remember the night Samara Elise greeted us. I was two days away from my due date, impatiently awaiting her arrival and whiling away time by bingeing Netflix shows. In the midst of a gory episode of *Marco Polo*, I felt the first set of contractions. The same as with the first, my labor proceeded quite quickly. I delivered her, also epidural-free, in the wee hours of March 15, 2015, only three hours after I checked into the hospital. She was a chunky baby with the squishiest cheeks and pink lips.

As Samara's personality traits started to emerge, I knew right away that she was going to be the ultimate mommy's girl. She followed me everywhere, first crawling and later on waddling to wherever I was in order to watch whatever I was doing. We had the same dominant characteristics. From early in her life, I noticed that she was fearless, territorial, protective, stubborn yet sensitive, compassionate, and loved with no holds barred.

Life with two babies was a major adjustment. With no help, it was just me and Andre running the household and tending to the kids.

During this time, I stumbled upon mom support groups on Facebook. I learned most of my parenting skills through experience, some through advice of family and friends and a good chunk through these support groups. We had local meetups and play dates, and became obsessed with buying matching, handmade clothing pieces for our girls.

The expansion of our family propelled us to purchase our first home, and in the midst of the moving chaos, working full-time, and raising two littles, life went by pretty much in a blur.

Toward the end of 2016, I got the biggest surprise when I found out we were pregnant again. This pregnancy mimicked all the symptoms of the previous one, and I was bedridden during my entire first trimester and a few weeks into the second. I was on round two of the incessant dry heaving and full-on regurgitations, the agonizing hospital admissions and dreaded needle pricks. To add to the fun, this was also my first bout with sciatica pain. Thankfully, it went away after birth.

I was scheduled for induction on October 7, as I was already past my due date. Around 10 p.m. on October 5, I felt the first set of the all too familiar labor pains. Based on my prior experience, I already knew my labor would go quickly from there.

True enough, I made it to the hospital with only a few minutes to spare until I had to push. After thirty minutes of pushing, which was the longest I experienced for all my babies, I was exhausted and could barely lift my head. Still, I stubbornly refused all offers for an epidural.

The doctor decided that I would have to undergo an emergency Caesarean section if the baby didn't come out in the next couple of minutes. Immediately, I went into panic mode. I had never experienced any major surgeries nor ever undergone anesthesia.

I mustered whatever was left of my physical strength and pushed and pushed with everything I had. Around 12:06 a.m. on October 6, 2017, as the new day began, Riley Amelia, my youngest child, marked her presence with the most ear-splitting screams. We found out that the umbilical cord had wrapped itself around her body, which prevented a smooth descent and prolonged the delivery. She came out on her own terms, completing our little family.

Riley was the gift I didn't know I needed but now cannot do without. The frosting on the cake, the cherry on top, the finishing touch that completes a piece of work.

In retrospect, Riley's arrival couldn't have been timed better. I was six years into motherhood, old enough to have gained some wisdom yet also young enough to be able to keep up with the physical demands of tending to a newborn plus two active children.

She was a colicky baby, and during those early days—or nights, rather—we truly got to know each other. It wasn't exactly the most pleasant of introductions. She cried her way into the morning while I recuperated from the battle scars of childbirth and handled the post-partum depression. There I was, a mother of three, supposedly seasoned yet feeling so utterly helpless, just trying my best to get through those nights. I would rock her to sleep while humming "Edelweiss," the only song that calmed her down. It was the aggregation of these factors that changed the game for me, ultimately sealing the deal that she would be our last child.

At the peak of my depression, I lost my zest for life. I couldn't make sense nor take control of the negative feelings that possessed me. I wanted to be alone in my room all the time, and I would burst out crying for no reason. For fear of being judged, I didn't tell anyone. My family and friends know me as someone who is put-together all the time. How would they react if they found out what was truly happening behind closed doors?

I had thoughts of harming myself and would call my company's Employee Assistance Counseling hotline seeking solace, as I felt my family would never understand. Then one day, I woke up with a different kind of feeling. Suddenly, everything was right in the world again. Without resorting to medication or taking proactive steps, the old me had reemerged. In researching, I learned that the timing coincidentally aligned with when my post-partum hormones were expected to balance out.

With eleven years of motherhood now under my belt, I've realized that being a mother is like belonging to a secret club of women who are simultaneously going through the same set of experiences, cutting across geography and social stature. It is a group ultimately bonded by the love they have for their children, which is all-consuming, overwhelming at times, reckless to a fault, and knows no reservations. When a baby is born, this kind of love ensues.

Motherhood is comprised of many moments of happiness followed by long stretches of blurry, repetitive days. It is the point at which all human emotions coalesce. An honor of the highest form that is transcendent, not transient. A lifelong challenge in which failure is never an option.

It comes with the realization that the thing that takes up so much of me is the very thing that keeps me going. It's crazy and beautiful and absolute.

One Day

As moonbeams slip through the window cracks,
I lie in bed, engulfed in deafening silence,
Interrupted only by the tossing and turning
of three little bodies
Deep in the bosom of sleep.
Another day has gone by.
Dusk makes way for dawn,
Then dawn for dusk.
Before long, I am thrust
Into the throes of silence once more.
But one day, there will be no more interruptions.
My heart breaks as it bursts.

—P. S. Angeles

Soul Starved

———◆•◆———

When Maxine was three months old, my best friend flew in from Manila to stand as godmother for her Catholic baptism. It was the first time we had seen each other as newly minted mothers; what used to be trips to the clubs were now replaced with visits to Target and Toys "R" Us.

While planning her itinerary, we decided to take this opportunity to have a girls' trip. I also happened to have available flight credit that I was wanting to use. We decided on New York City, since it was somewhat close by and neither of us had been there.

Andre was fully supportive, I suspect because he'd seen me go through the pains of pregnancy and childbirth, added to the fact that I contracted Bell's

Palsy hours after I delivered Maxine. We all thought I was experiencing the early signs of a stroke due to the trauma my body had just endured, but it turned out to be a viral infection that caused temporary facial paralysis on the right side of my face. It took a full four weeks of round-the-clock medication and acupuncture sessions before I finally saw some semblance of healing, which made for a very depressing time. My self-confidence plummeted to rock bottom, and I questioned my abilities as a new mother. How was I supposed to care for this tiny human being while also taking care of myself? Eating was pure torture, and I had to use a straw for drinking and an eye patch for sleeping because my affected eye couldn't close all the way.

Having witnessed all of that, Andre knew I needed this break. Reluctantly, I left Maxine in his more-than-capable hands, mom-guilt coursing through me. The planning phase and the idea of a trip had been fun, but the act of leaving was harder than I thought. However, I justified my decision by convincing myself that maybe, just maybe, I would emerge as a mentally healthier and therefore, happier and better mother after all this.

For three days, I missed Maxine dearly. But, as it turned out, my soul needed this trip. Motherhood, in all its wonderful glory, has a tendency to consume us, and if you have a faint heart, it will eat you alive.

In fact, there came a point when I truly believed that without it, I hardly knew myself. I couldn't decipher the line separating motherhood and me. Did I equal motherhood and vice versa? Without motherhood, was there anything more to me?

Sometimes, it is self-discovery trips like this one that enable us to refocus and remind us of our core. They help us see that if we strip away motherhood, we are *not* nothing.

Modern Parenting

In retracing my childhood and the ways in which I was raised, I often find distinct differences between how I am raising my own kids and what I experienced growing up. There is, give or take, a thirty-year age gap from when I was my eldest daughter's current age.

Back then, the only technological concern parents had to contend with was the regulation of TV time. Before the days of cable television, kids much preferred to play outside. Physical activity wasn't an issue, unlike today, where schools have to mindfully allocate time for brain breaks, which often translates into stretches, dancing, or anything that involves moving your body.

As part of routine appointments, medical providers now have to check that kids are getting the recommended amount of time engaging in physical activity each day. The proliferation of gadgets specifically targeted to children seems to be doing more harm than good. I struggle with limiting gadget time for the kids, and it bothers me when Andre and I are both busy and we end up literally leaving them to their own devices.

Directly correlated to this is how my daughters are being raised in a world where everything is in excess. Unlimited food choices, too much sugar, overstimulation of gadgets—everything is designed to cater to convenience and instant gratification. Today's environment offers little opportunity to practice patience. To be resourceful. To wait.

Most everything is sugar coated. And even if our intentions are noble, wanting to spare them from hurt or pain, we are actually doing them a disservice.

When Maxine was three, she was gifted her first pet, a goldfish that she fittingly named Coral. One day, she approached me, her little face looking so forlorn, and said that her fish looked sick and needed to be brought to the hospital for a shot.

I asked her, "What makes you say that?"

She took my hand and led me to the fish bowl, confirming what I already knew. Coral was gone.

For a moment, I grappled with words while thinking of the best way to approach this situation. How do I explain the facts truthfully to a three-year-old without muddling her thoughts and resorting to fake euphemisms like "she went to fish heaven"?

In the end, I settled on something along the lines of, "She is really sick, and there's nothing we or the animal doctors can do to save her. The best thing we can do is to send her back to the ocean where she belongs." And together, we flushed Coral's lifeless body down the toilet bowl.

I then realized that, coincidentally, fish have been part of two very crucial moments of my life, causing me to ponder things I otherwise would not have: peer pressure and now, death. From broaching the subject of death at six years old, here I was, now on the other side of the fence, figuring out how to best introduce it to my own child. Life had come full circle.

Whenever there is an opportunity, I try to teach my children negative concepts such as loss, suffering, hardship, tragedy, and the like. I want them to reflect on these hard truths and have realistic expectations of the world and of the people they will encounter. As much as we love our fairytales, real life isn't always about happy endings. The last thing I want is for them to grow up in a bubble, completely out of touch with reality, ill-equipped to cope with adversity. The day that happens is the day I will have failed them.

During moments of self-contemplation, I often wonder how I am faring at parenting so far. Am I doing enough? Am I being too harsh? How do I extend my patience? Do my kids feel how much I love them?

Some questions we will never get answers to. With parenting, there are no do-overs, but on rare occasions, you are gifted with second chances. Sometimes, this comes through a completely different scenario but an equally perfect opportunity to achieve the same result. Occasionally, we encounter one-and-dones. These are the hardest to accept, but all we can do is try our best and let go.

Despite the mounting expectations around parenting in this day and age, I remain steadfast about my golden rule. It took me a while to figure it out, but it's really quite simple. Of the list of dreams we have for our children, which one takes precedence above all? For me, it is their genuine happiness. Since that realization, I make a conscious effort every day to ask my kids if they are happy. Some days, I don't have to ask because I'll get my answer in the form of nonverbal cues like their squeals of delight and their little dances, or through their faces lit up in pure excitement. These, for me, are the best days.

Too Good

———◆•◆———

Sometime in 2015, after the birth of Samara, I ended up in a Facebook group for online job seekers. During the course of my search, one company stood out from the rest.

Bored and curious, I went to their website and saw this flashy video of a social mixer at an exotic location: overflowing drinks, scantily clad partygoers, drone shots, EDM pounding in the background. It was supposed to be a networking event-slash-big-celebration of the company's top producers.

Digging deeper on the website, I discovered that they advertised themselves as a multimedia marketing company. To join, you had to pay for and complete modules aimed to teach you about the basics of jump-starting an online business and the effective marketing strategies to keep it afloat. Upon completion, you would be assigned a coach, who would then provide step-by-step guidance on getting your business established.

The more I researched it, the more interested I became. I paid for the modules and completed the courses diligently. I was assigned my first coach, a lady by the name of Chelsea. After completing my sessions with her, I advanced to a more senior coach named Andy. These senior coaches are said to be the best of the best, the top producers of the company.

I looked up Andy's background, and he appeared to be a real person who apparently had written a book about business strategy development. I attended my first session with him online. The topic was about taking risks to reap great rewards, how you have to sometimes gamble your way to financial stability. We were left with an assignment and asked to contact him once we were ready for the next steps.

I finished my work that weekend and immediately notified him. At this point, we had not seen each other face-to-face; all communication was done through a messaging app. When I stated that I was ready to move forward, I was greeted with a great deal of excitement, which, in turn, amped up my own excitement as well.

He then talked about different levels of marketing packages I could choose from. These resembled a starter kit of what one would need to launch a business. Each level differed significantly in price point. I told him I was going with the most basic package, the cheapest one that included only the essentials. I just wanted to try it out; if things didn't work out, I found this amount an acceptable financial loss.

I could tell right away just by his messages how the tone then changed. His responses started to lack excitement, and somehow, he even seemed irate!

He went on to "encourage" me to go for the top tier, which I declined, telling him I didn't have that kind of liquid money. He began to work harder at trying to convince me, saying they had partnered with a reputable financial services company that had helped entrepreneurs fund their start-up businesses. He delivered this information in a way that was very convincing, showing me testimonials and success stories. Before I knew it, I was lured in by the promise of sweet success.

I've always been a risk-taker. And that applies to all aspects of my life. So, before knowing fully what I was getting into, I took a gamble.

At this stage, I had already been forewarned by some family members that it all sounded very suspicious, but I ignored their admonitions, and soon enough, I signed the documents for a "business loan" in the form of multiple credit cards. I was coached to use these cards to establish my own website and create a funnel that would direct all marketing package sales to Andy, who would also get a commission for every website sign-up.

I went all-in, secured my own website domain, and then hired a graphic designer and a videographer to create my own video advertisement to place on my site. I made a dedicated Instagram account, pushing content tirelessly every day. I paid for social media traffic to "increase" my online presence and sent automated emails to my personal and professional contacts, basically asking for their business.

A few weeks into this gig, I was running on autopilot. Everything was set up, and all I had to do was wait for the money to kick in. I gave it some more time, and when I still wasn't getting any traction, I attempted to contact my coaches to ask for some advice.

I was shocked (and also, in a way, not shocked) to find out they had blocked me as a contact. And then it dawned on me. It was all too good to be true. I had turned a blind eye to every red flag I'd come across, stubbornly believing that this was going to be my big break.

Dejected, I did my due diligence. Had I only done it earlier in the process, I could have avoided this dilemma. As it turned out, the company was fictitious, and the bigshot coaches were really just sales people trained to milk money out of gullible people like me. It was your typical pyramid scheme hidden under the pretense of a tried-and-tested business model of successful entrepreneurship, suggesting it was bound to take off and, once automated, would yield passive income.

How very cunning of them and so very naive of me. I'd heard horror stories of people falling victim to similar financial scams, and being in the banking world, I was no stranger to this. But I still somehow fell prey.

I found myself in major debt thanks to this blunder, and I had no clue how to get out of it. Then it hit me. What if I had just compromised my children's future? What if it was all downhill from here? After months of strategizing, I ended up pooling my savings to pay off some of the smaller cards. But it still wasn't enough.

Lollie, notorious for saving me from sticky situations, ended up bailing me out of the rest of my debt. Fortunately, I did not have to declare bankruptcy or end up selling major possessions, but it was a hard-earned lesson. I am now more vigilant, and whenever I encounter get-rich-quick schemes, I steer clear.

About three years after this incident, a news exposé came out regarding the company and how the owners had tried to scam so many others like me. A case was filed against them by the Federal Trade Commission, and after an arduous litigation process, a settlement was reached. I received a check in the mail—not quite the total amount I'd lost, but enough to help ease the heartbreak.

The big takeaway here, which is something I knew all along but chose to ignore, is if it's too good to be true, it probably is.

A Pain in
the Bum

———— ✦ ————

O n my thirty-seventh birthday, my sciatica pain returned with a vengeance. I felt the now-familiar excruciating pain in my left side that radiated from my coccyx bone all the way to my toe. I was brought to urgent care, administered a steroid shot, and prescribed a slew of oral medications to reduce the inflammation and help me manage the pain. I got better gradually, but after eight months, I woke up to a full-blown flare-up in the middle of the night. I couldn't get up without flipping onto my stomach and crawling off the bed. Simple movements would cause torturous pain, and I struggled to fulfill my daily tasks.

I was once again ordered another round of the same medications and remained bedridden while I let my body heal. What hurt more than the physical pain was the deterioration of my quality of life. I was unable to carry, bathe, and play with my kids like I normally would. I couldn't sit upright on my work chair for more than five minutes. Driving was out of the question, and I was facilitating meetings while lying in only either supine or prone positions, my laptop beside me. Upon my doctor's recommendation, I cancelled our long-planned trip to the Fiji Islands, where we were supposed to renew our wedding vows. The ten-hour flight would be too taxing on my back.

I avoided all social contact, staying hunkered down in my room as I once again battled bouts of anxiety and depression.

In an attempt to sever my dependence on pain medications, I decided to seek alternative treatments while also trying to get to the root of the issue. I needed a treatment plan that would target the underlying cause of my condition rather than the symptoms. After seeing a Physical Medicine specialist and undergoing x-rays and an MRI exam, I was diagnosed as having two bulging discs in the lumbar area, specifically in the L4-5 and L5-S1.

The wear and tear of my spine resulted from an accumulation of factors: a stagnant lifestyle (no regular exercise and lack of physical activity), the nature of my work (desk job for fifteen years), the trauma of back-to-back childbirths, and genetics (my dad was diagnosed with the same exact condition at the same exact age).

I underwent physical therapy, IV therapy, physiotherapy, acupuncture, and went to a chiropractor for adjustments and traction therapy. Simultaneously, I took cannabidoil (CBD) edibles to help with pain management. The combination of these treatments eventually sped up my healing, and as my range of motion improved, my lifestyle slowly went back to normal.

How quickly things can change in the blink of an eye. One day, you're young and invincible, acting purely upon impulse without a care for your body and well-being, and then things like this happen causing paradigm shifts and drastic lifestyle changes while you hope against hope that it's not yet too late.

To Have It All

———◆•◆———

Thirty-eight years of existence. I know I still have a long journey ahead of me, but I want to pause and reflect at the midpoint of my life and assess my learnings so far.

Growing up, my eyes were on my dad, who set the benchmark of personhood so incredibly high that I'm inclined never to settle for second best. This is the ideal upon which my personal philosophy was born: the pursuit of perfection as an end unto itself.

I was watching the series *Sex Life* recently and the episode was about people who want to have it all.

How that is not possible, how "100%" is a myth, and we should settle for "80%" or risk losing it all.

This may be true in love and relationships—on a case-by-case basis. But if we apply this ideal to everything else in life, I don't know that I agree. What if, in our quest to reach that 100%, we attain an additional 10%, and our 80% now becomes 90%? Isn't that considered a win? But the bigger question here though is, how much are you willing to risk?

I don't want to live a mediocre life. I want to experience it all and have no regrets when I am lying on my deathbed. Andre often chides me, saying that this kind of mentality will send me to an early grave. I shrug it off each time, but I know I wouldn't have it any other way.

There is a Post-it note taped to my computer monitor with the words, "Try better every day." Not only is it a reminder to stay aligned with my personal philosophy, but it is also a testament, an acceptance that I am flawed, as we all are. One of our defining qualities as human beings is resilience. How do we respond to failure? How do we bounce back from mistakes? Some days this is easier said than done. On these days, we are allowed to sulk. Bask in our misery. But at some point, we must keep on going.

With this in mind, and through the recollection of stories in this book, I can't help but contemplate: What has my existence brought forth up to this halfway stage of my life? What can I do to improve the next phase? Has my life been a triumph or a tragedy so far? Or is it both all at once because perhaps one cannot exist without the other?

After all, aren't most of history's triumphs born in some way out of loss, suffering, or other forms of sacrifice? Perhaps it is neither, yet. To be determined, as the rest of my stories have yet to unfold.

Until then, my journey to the endpoint continues.

Travel
Adventures

MIDPOINT EDITION

*Thirty-Eight Notable Adventures
in Thirty-Eight Years*

✓ Spending summer holidays as a child in Ocean Park in Hong Kong.

✓ Crossing the Hong Kong border to explore Shenzhen, China, by bike.

✓ Reveling in wide-eyed wonder at the beauty of Angkor Wat in Siem Reap, Cambodia.

✓ Admiring Osaka Castle and taking strolls along the many alleys and back streets in Asakusa, Japan.

✓ Paying homage to the architecturally beautiful, iconic temples in Bangkok, Thailand.

✓ Dancing without a care in the world at Zouk in Clarke Quay, Singapore.

✓ Ringing in the New Year decked in four layers of clothes at the Las Vegas Strip in the company of friends, fireworks, and overflowing booze.

✓ Taking on the Diamond Head hiking trail on a whim in flip-flops and a mini skirt, while in O'ahu, Hawaii.

✓ Driving around Miami, Florida without a map or GPS and stumbling upon a nude beach.

✓ Purchasing a hundred dollars' worth of merchandise to queue for a photo opportunity with Candice Swanepoel at the Victoria's Secret flagship store in Herald Square in New York.

✓ Completing a scavenger hunt by foot with co-workers around Charlotte, North Carolina.

✓ Celebrating hard-fought victories with my team during happy hour on scenic Amelia Island, Florida.

✓ Wading in an underground river in Cancun, Mexico.

✓ Visiting Bob Marley's childhood home and eating authentic jerk chicken in the mountains of Nine Mile, Jamaica.

✓ Riding a catamaran through Stingray City in the Cayman Islands.

✓ Zip-lining drenched from head to toe in an unstoppable downpour in Roatan, Honduras.

✓ Climbing atop a Mayan ruin in Altun Ha in Belize.

✓ Getting serenaded during a gondola ride and downing Jägerbombs at Piazza San Marco in Venice, Italy.

✓ Sailing through the beautiful coastline of Dubrovnik, Croatia.

✓ Witnessing breathtaking sunsets and endless shades of blue and white around the village of Oia in Santorini, Greece.

✓ Driving up the mountainside in a 4 x 4 Jeep with manual transmission in Corfu, Greece.

✓ Partying on Halloween with strangers while aboard a cruise ship in the middle of the Adriatic Sea.

✓ Overindulging on Sprüngli chocolate and feasting on raclette aboard a fondue tram in Zurich, Switzerland.

✓ Meeting Yul Kwon at Disney Aulani Resort in Ko'Olina, Hawai'i.

✓ Soaking up the sun at the Atlantis resort in Nassau, Bahamas.

✓ Building sandcastles on Disney's private island, Castaway Cay.

✓ Getting lost in Ensenada, Mexico, and eating at the first restaurant we chanced upon—a McDonald's.

✓ Guzzling beer at Nyhavn 17 in Copenhagen, Denmark.

✓ Chasing the kids around Skansen, an open-air museum and zoo on the island of Djurgården in Stockholm, Sweden.

✓ Witnessing the cityscape from 933 feet atop the Columbia Center in Seattle, Washington.

✓ Literally and figuratively stopping to smell the flowers at the Butchart Gardens in British Columbia, Canada.

- ✓ Celebrating St. Patrick's Day on the streets of Dublin, Ireland.

- ✓ Visiting the Game of Thrones filming locations and shooting arrows on GOT sets in the United Kingdom.

- ✓ Rushing to the airport, two young kids and a baby in tow, only to miss our flight to Liverpool, England.

- ✓ Transporting a Christmas tree and a big box of decorations to our Airbnb in Joshua Tree, where we welcomed Christmas Day during the peak of a pandemic.

- ✓ Getting stuck in our cabin during a snow storm up in the mountains of Green Valley Lake.

- ✓ Swimming beside giant honu green sea turtles, in Waikoloa, Hawai'i.

- ✓ Visiting six theme parks in five days in Orlando, Florida while struggling to stay cool in scorching triple-digit temperatures.

Acknowledgments

It takes a village to produce a book, and I'd be remiss if I did not properly express my gratitude to everyone who made *Midpoint* possible.

My editor, Kathryn Galán of Wynnpix Productions, for teaching me the ropes of the complicated world of book writing and publishing, for her endless patience, and for taking a chance on me. I did just about everything to drive her nuts, still she remained unfazed.

Maithy Vu, who helped with developmental edits. It is an honor to have some traces of you in my book.

Susan Gaigher, for being the consummate professional whose meticulous eye helped polish my work.

My cover-designer, the talented Sebastian Cudicio. I envisioned a cover that was minimalist yet heavy on symbolism and Sebastian came through.

Ksenija Petranovic for the beautiful interior illustrations.

Shelby Gates for her help and expertise in formatting the interior pages and delivering an overall cohesive look which was my only request.

Dr. Issam Ghazzawi, my former MBA professor and mentor, for his continued support and for his generosity in writing the foreword of this book.

Atty. Robert Pimm for his time and invaluable legal advice.

Marilen Mendoza, for my author photo.

Stephanie Hoogstad, Susan Griggs, Jordan Tate, Rachel White, and Danny Raye who performed beta reading services and whose detailed feedback and critique helped refine my manuscript.

My friends Arlene and Marjorie, the only two souls outside my immediate family who knew about this book during its infancy. Thank you for your friendship, encouragement, and support.

My parents, Janet and Ding, for raising us in a home that never lacked in love and laughter, and for instilling the value of family. I hope I've made you both proud.

To my siblings, Bryan, Marvin, and Timmy, for the best childhood I could ever hope for, one that produced the most solid core memories, which I will carry with me forever.

To my aunt and godmother, Joy, my second mother, who was an inspiration to me while growing up. Thank you to you, Tito Henry, and cousins Miles and Jessica, for sharing your home with me and my family, to help us kick-start our life in the U.S.

My grandmother Raymunda, for molding me into the person I am today. For tirelessly bailing me out of sticky situations. For supporting me in every endeavor and every pursuit I set my sights on. You gave me all the tools I needed to be successful in life. A huge part of what I am today is because of you.

My mother-in-law, Cherry, for toasting to my successes and encouraging me to keep writing.

To my husband, Andre, for his unceasing support, for constantly pushing me out of my comfort zone, and for being the one who believed in this book even before it came to fruition. My #1 silent cheerleader, happy and content in the sidelines while I chase my crazy and superfluous ambitions. Thank you for holding down the fort while I was buried in edits upon edits. Because of you and your sacrifices, I get to live my wildest dreams.

To my children, Max, Sam, and Riley, my life's greatest reward times three and the antithesis of every poor choice and wrong turn I've made in my journey. Because of you, I am inspired to try harder, to push more, to live a little (sometimes a lot!). For being my best teachers and the reason why I have decided to write this book. Thank you for tethering me to the things that truly matter. This, as with everything else I do, is for you.

Lastly, if you or a loved one is experiencing emotional distress or going through a suicidal crisis, please call or text the Suicide and Crisis Lifeline at 988.

Author Q&A

What inspired you to write this book?

As mentioned in the Preface, I wanted to leave a tangible legacy to my daughters and show them a side of me that they have not been privy to, since they only see and know me as *Mom*. That was always my main intent and what prompted me to finally kick-start this passion project.

Can you tell me about this book?

Midpoint is a collection of stories starting from my childhood and going up to the present, noting major milestones of my life, memories and experiences that have made an impact, and influential figures who have molded me into the kind of person I am today.

What was the most challenging part of writing this book?

For me, it was working to present my stories in a seamless manner. I struggled with chronology, as some of the story timelines overlapped. I had to be creative in weaving them all together in order for everything to flow smoothly. Countless times, I had to rearrange the chapters, making sure each one connected sensibly with the next.

What does the title mean?

Midpoint is meant to signify that I've reached the literal halfway point of life, based on the average human lifespan, and regardless of any factor that might impact that. I wanted to pause and assess my learnings so far and then apply whatever those were to improve (or at least try to!) the second half of my life.

What can readers hope to learn from this book?

This book was written with my daughters in mind the whole time. If it ends up in other people's hands, the one takeaway I hope they leave with is the importance and power of stories, because what are we but an accumulation of our experiences? When we bequeath these to our children, they become stories; all together, it becomes our legacy.

Praise for Midpoint

Writing for your daughters and finishing your work against odds will always be an inspiration to others.

—GINA APOSTOL
Best-Selling Author of "Insurrecto"

It was such a pleasure reading Midpoint. Patricia's resilience was present throughout these stories, and I so admire her philosophy and strength.

—MAITHY VU
Editor and Author of Best-Selling Book "Rebel Girls"

I really enjoyed this book. Patricia has a unique perspective that I believe readers will value, and I came away with a deeper respect for her accomplishments.

— SUSAN GRIGGS,
Beta Reader

This memoir is very well-written. It is entirely truthful, not pulling any punches. The conclusion is one of the best I have seen in my time as a beta reader of nonfiction pieces. People tend to just summarize the earlier content, so it's nice to see a book that ends on a more forward-looking note.

— STEPHANIE HOOGSTAD
Beta Reader

Patricia is a great writer with a good instinct for pacing and flow. Her succinct approach is very refreshing.

— SUSAN GAIGHER
Editor

Midpoint has quite a lot of potential to help a large number of people. The life advice given paired with the interesting stories will make anyone eager to read it!

— JORDAN TATE
Beta Reader